Keto Airfryer Cookbook For Two

Easy Ketogenic Recipes With Your Removable Air Fryer Lid

BARB SWINDOLL

Copyright © 2019 **Barb Swindoll**

All rights reserved. No part of this publication may be reproduced, distributed, or transmitted in any form or by any means, including photocopying, recording, or other electronic or mechanical methods, without the prior written permission of the publisher, except in the case of brief quotations embodied in critical reviews and certain other noncommercial uses permitted by copyright law.

Limit of Liability/Disclaimer of Warranty: While the publisher and author have used their best efforts in preparing this book, they make no representations or warranties with respect to the accuracy or completeness of the contents of this book and specifically disclaim any implied warranties of merchantability or fitness for a particular purpose. No warranty may be created or extended by sales representatives or written sales materials. The advice and strategies contained herein may not be suitable for your situation. You should consult with a professional where appropriate. Neither the publisher nor author shall be liable for any loss of profit or any other commercial damages, including but not limited to special, incidental, consequential, or other damages.

ISBN: 9798627509969

DEDICATION

Thank you Ray, for 10 years of pleasurable memories!

TABLE OF CONTENTS

INTRODUCTION 1

BREAKFAST 5

    Asparagus Cheese Frittata 6

    Crispy Bacon 7

    Kale and Feta Frittatas 8

    Buttery Onion Tofu Scramble 9

    Breakfast Frittata 10

    Scotch Eggs With Spicy Sauce 11

    Spicy Bacon Breakfast 12

    Crispy Herb And Cheese Frittata 13

    Air Fried Breakfast Sausage 14

    Baked Egg Cups With Spinach & Cheese 15

    Egg And Cheese Scramble 16

PORK 17

    Air Fryer Pork Loin 18

    BBQ Pork Chops 19

    Vietnamese Pork Noodle 20

    Breaded Pork Chops 22

    Parmesan Crusted Pork Chops 23

BEEF 25

    Salisbury Steak Burgers 26

    Air Fryer Hamburgers 27

    Super Easy Steak 29

    Keto Meatloaf Sliders 30

Beef Kheema Meatloaf 31

Juicy Crispy Steak 32

POULTRY 33

Pop Almond Chicken 34

Keto Crisp Chicken 35

Baked Chicken Nuggets 37

Chicken Wings With Buffalo Sauce 39

Asian Barbecue Satay 41

Crispy Garlic Ranch Wings 42

Turkish Chicken Bites 43

Crispy Sausage Dinner 44

Tandoori Chicken 45

Buffalo Chicken Meatballs 47

Keto Drumsticks 48

Chicken Coconut Meatballs 49

Brazilian Chicken 50

Crispy Chicken Nuggets 53

    Butter Chicken With Broccoli 54

Whole Roast Chicken 55

Keto Air Fried Chicken 57

Keto Adobo Chicken Thighs 58

Air Fried Turkey Breast 60

FISH & SEAFOOD 63

Salmon Yoghurt Fillets 64

Crispy Breaded Fish Sticks 65

Sesame Fish 66

- Air-Fried Shrimp Scampi 67
- Coconut Shrimp 68
- Cajun Butter Baked Salmon 69
- Cajun Shrimp 71

VEGETABLES 73
- Thai Shrimp Salad 74
- Tomato Basil Scallops 75
- Creamed Spinach 77
- Asian Sesame Ginger Broccoli 78
- Crispy Moroccan Chickpeas 80
- Asparagus Fries With Aioli 81
- Paneer And Cheese Veg Cutlet 83

APPETIZERS & SNACKS 85
- Crispy Jalapeno Coins 86
- Bacon Wrapped Asparagus 87
- Roasted Turnips 88
- Jalapeno Sausage Poppers 89
- Zucchini Pasta 90
- Crispy Kale Chips 91
- Grilled Cheese 92
- Air Fried Blooming Onion 93
- Air Fried Cabbage 94
- Crispy Spinach 95
- Radish Hash Browns 96
- Spicy Cabbage 97
- Crispy Avocado Fries 98

Scotch- Pork Ring Style Eggs 99

Zucchini Chips 100

Crispy Brussels Sprouts 101

Balsamic Asparagus With Almonds 102

Cheese Sticks 103

Air Fryer Biscuits 104

Keto Onion Rings 105

Quick &Easy Air-Fried Asparagus 106

Roasted Broccoli 107

INTRODUCTION

Congratulations on your purchase of this book. It promises to be an exciting and fulfilling journey, I assure you. Not only will you be enjoying great tasty ketogenic meals, you will be preparing them in an excitingly new way via your Removable Crispy lid, and savoring every moment! You are set for quick and easy cooking. Using the Crispy Lid is easy, and since you will be cooking just for two, you can always put together the ingredients that are mostly readily available.

The idea of cooking for two is essential. When on a keto diet, your family do not have to be on that journey with you, at least not all the time. Give them a break and keep them from sighing "Oh not…Not another keto meal!" Don't get me wrong. The Keto diet is awesome. Otherwise, I won't be writing about it. This is a diet that has been proven to be very effective against many illnesses and diseases that people regularly struggle with. It aids weight loss and helps to maintain optimum health. The ketogenic diet is an ultra-low carbohydrate and high fat diet that is different from other low carb eating because its primary focus is to change the body's energy source to ketones, instead of carbohydrate. This diet promotes the eating of fresh, whole foods like fish, meat, dairy, eggs, green vegetables as well as healthy fats and oils. You and partner will be better for it!

Additionally, Crispy Lid cooking is quantity cooking. The fryer basket, like many other air fryers, are not designed to hold large amounts of ingredients. This is why many people using the air fryer, cook in batches. But if cooking just for two, cooking in batches is significantly reduced, or even eliminated. Every modern kitchen needs to have the Crispy lid. It turns your electric pressure cooker into an air fryer. Many people love pressure cooking and air frying and it is a magical that manufacturers would come up with a revolutionary appliance like this, to bridge the gap between these two cooking modes. Now you can finish off your pressure cooked foods by air frying them, or simply air frying them, providing your meals with that crispiness and crunchiness that you desire.

Its ease of use is unparalleled. The Crisp Lid works with any electric pressure cooker of 6 quart or 8 quart. So your options are varied. You can use any multi-cooker that can fit. It has only 6 buttons and presets with which you set the temperature and the cook time, increase and decrease them as necessary and of course, the Stop and Start cook button. Unlike regular airfryers with maximum cooking temperature of 400°F, this removable device can be adjusted to a maximum temperature of 500°F, helping to deliver well-broiled meats, amongst others.

It is so easy to cook in. Just place the trivet in the stainless steel inner pot of your pressure cooker. Place your basket or pan on top of the trivet. Place the device on the pot and simply plug in. Ensure the lid handle is firmly in the Down position. Use the controls to set and adjust the temperature and cook time. The Crisp Lid also has a transparent glass lid that helps you to see and monitor inside the food as it cooks. This makes cooking even easier as you do not need to take out the lid to check your progress. However, it shouldn't be touched, as it gets very hot!

For a reasonable sum, you can get your Removable Lid. It cost less than half of most air fryers in the market. It is convenient, safe to use and easy to store. It is versatile. It single-handedly turns your Pressure Cooker into an Air Fryer, performing multiple functions of crisping, broiling and air-frying your foods. It is quick; even quicker than using a conventional oven. It even performs the function of a grill. It is a one-pot experience that you will enjoy. Safety is guaranteed on account of its various safety precautions while it is being used. For instance, it can only work when the handle is down in place. This guard against accidental switch-ons and burns.

When you buy the Crispy Lid, you also get some accessories to aid your cooking. These includes:

- A 3-inch trivet: to ensure the food is as close as possible to the heating element that's on the lid.
- An air-fryer basket: This holds the ingredients to be cooked.
- Stainless steel tongs: to remove the basket, or to shake and flip food around.
- A silicon trivet: To place the hot Crispy Lid immediately when removed.
- A user manual and a recipe booklet: for a more detailed instructions and user guide.

The manual provides all that you need to know about usage, safety and troubleshooting. See that you thoroughly read through before using. In this book, however, we will be showing you many ways to cook a meal. So if one way doesn't work for you, the other might. They are carefully selected to keep you in ketosis, and carefully selected to deliver a satisfactory experience.

Happy Cooking!

BREAKFAST

Asparagus Cheese Frittata

Less than 30 minutes of a healthy combination of Asparagus, Swiss cheese and cream, and the result is a creamy breakfast meal!

Prep Time: 10 minutes

Cook Time: 20 minutes

Servings: 2

Ingredients

1/4 lb. asparagus, trimmed & cut into 2 pieces each

1/4 cup green onions, chopped

½ tablespoon of butter

3eggs, whisked

1/8 cup heavy whipping cream

¼ cup grated Swiss cheese

½ teaspoon ground black pepper

½ teaspoon salt

Instructions

1. Steam the asparagus in1-2 tablespoons of water until tender. Remove and set to one side.

2. Combine the whisked egg, cheese, milk, the salt and the pepper in a bowl. Set to one side.

3. Add the chopped green onions to a pan. Cover with butter. Place the pan on the trivet and set the Crisp Lid on the inner steel pot of the pressure cooker and plug in.

4. Cook 2 minutes, remove Crisp Lid and place on silicon mat. Add the steamed asparagus, and the eggs mix to cover the vegetables. Plug in Crisp Lid.

5. Set temperature to 350°F and cook 15 minutes until cooked through.

6. Cut the frittata into four wedges and serve. Enjoy!

Nutritional Information Per Serving

Calories - 264, Carbohydrates – 4g, Fat – 21g, Proteins – 16g, Fiber – 2g

Crispy Bacon
Everyone loves bacon; let alone a crispy one!

Prep Time: 1 minute

Cook Time: 10 minutes

Servings: 2

Ingredients

6 bacon slices, no-sugar added

Instructions

1. Place in fryer basket. Place trivet in pot. Place basket on it. Set the Crisp Lid on the inner steel pot of the pressure cooker and plug in.

2. Cook at 400°F for 10minutes, flipping halfway through

Nutritional Information Per Serving

Calories - 90, Carbohydrates – 0g, Fat – 8g, Proteins – 6g, Fiber – 0g

Kale and Feta Frittatas

A beneficial way to make use of your veggies!

Prep Time: 5minutes

Cook Time: 10 minutes

Servings: 2

Ingredients

4 eggs

1 cup chopped kale

3 tablespoon of crumbled feta cheese

Salt and pepper

Instructions

1. Add together all the ingredients in a baking pan. Mix well to combine.

2. Place trivet in pot. Place pan on it. Set the Crisp Lid on the inner steel pot of the pressure cooker and plug in.

3. Cook at 360F for 5- 10minutes.

Nutritional Information Per Serving

Calories - 212, Carbohydrates – 5g, Fat – 13g, Proteins – 19g, Fiber – 1g

Buttery Onion Tofu Scramble

Prep Time: 5minutes

Cook Time: 8 minutes

Servings: 2

Ingredients

2 blocks of tofu, cut into cubes

4 tablespoons of butter

Black pepper & salt

1 cup of cheddar cheese, grated

2 medium- sized onions, sliced

Instructions

1. Combine the black pepper, salt and tofu in a bowl.

2. Sauté butter and onions for 3 minutes and then add the seasoned tofu. Let it cook for 2-3 minutes.

3. Transfer to pan. Add the cheddar cheese. Place trivet in pot. Place pan on it. Set the Crisp Lid on the inner steel pot of the pressure cooker and plug in.

4. Cook at 350°F for 10 minutes. Serve and enjoy hot.

Nutritional Information Per Serving

Calories - 586, Carbohydrates – 8g, Fat – 51g, Proteins – 23g, Fiber – 1g

Breakfast Frittata

Easy- to- make frittatas become even easier with a Crisp Lid. Simply use a cake pan lined with parchment paper and you're good to go!

Prep time: 15minutes

Cook time: 20minutes

Servings: 2

Ingredients

1/4 lb. breakfast sausage, cooked &crumbled

4 eggs, beaten lightly

1/2 cup of Cheddar-Monterey Jack blend, shredded

1 green onion, chopped

2 tablespoons of red bell pepper, diced

1 pinch of cayenne pepper powder (optional)

Cooking spray

Instructions

1. In a bowl, add together the eggs, sausage, bell pepper, Cheddar-Monterey Jack cheese, cayenne and onion and mix well to combine.

2. Spray a nonstick cake pan of 6x2-inches with cooking spray. Transfer the egg mixture to it.

3. Place trivet in pot. Place pan on it. Set the Crisp Lid on the inner steel pot of the pressure cooker and plug in.

4. Cook at 360°F for 20 minutes or until the frittata is set.

Nutritional Information Per Serving

Calories - 380, Carbohydrates – 2.9g, Fat – 27.4g, Proteins – 31.2g, Fiber

Scotch Eggs With Spicy Sauce

A delicious, grease-free dish!

Prep time: 20 minutes

Cook time: 25 minutes

Servings: 2

Ingredients

8 oz. pork sausage

½ tablespoon fresh chives, finely chopped

1 tablespoons fresh parsley, finely chopped

Pinch nutmeg, freshly grated

Pinch ground black pepper

1 Pinch salt

2 hard-cooked eggs, peeled

½ cup Parmesan cheese, shredded

1 teaspoon coarse-ground mustard

Instructions

1. Add together the sausage, chives, nutmeg, mustard, parsley, salt, and black pepper in a bowl. Mix gently and shape into 2 patties of equal sizes.

2. Place each of the egg on a sausage patty. Shape the sausage around the egg and then dip in the parmesan cheese to coat well.

3. Place the eggs in the fryer basket. Spritz with oil. Place trivet in pot. Place basket on it. Set the Crisp Lid on the inner steel pot of the pressure cooker and plug in.

4. Set temperature to 400°F for 15 minutes, flipping halfway and spritzing again with oil. Enjoy with coarse-ground mustard.

Nutritional Information Per Serving

Calories - 909, Carbohydrates – 12g, Fat – 58g, Proteins – 86g, Fiber – 2g

Spicy Bacon Breakfast
A 10-minute healthy breakfast that's perfect for all.

Prep Time: 2 minutes

Cook Time: 10 minutes

Servings: 2-3

Ingredients

6 bacon slices

1/4 teaspoon allspice seasoning

1 tablespoon of splenda

1/4 teaspoon crushed red pepper flakes

Instructions

1. Combine all the spice mixture in a bowl. Dredge the bacon slices in the mix to coat well.

2. Transfer to the air fryer basket. Place the basket on the trivet and place trivet in pot. Place the Crisp Lid on top of the inner pot and plug it in.

3. Set temperature to 350°F and timer for 8 minutes. Flip halfway and keep cooking until crisp.

Nutritional Information Per Serving

Calories - 81, Carbohydrates – 0g, Fat – 7g, Proteins – 5g, Fiber – 0g

Crispy Herb And Cheese Frittata

Delicious and easy breakfast option

Prep time: 10minutes

Cook time: 15minutes

Servings: 2

Ingredients

4 eggs

1/2 cup half and half

1/3 cup cheddar cheese, shredded

2 tablespoons green scallions, chopped

2 tablespoons cilantro or parsley, chopped

1/2 teaspoon salt

1/2 teaspoon ground pepper

Instructions

1. Grease a 6-inch pan and whisk the eggs together in a bowl, together with the half and half.

2. Add the rest of the ingredients. Place the trivet in the pot and then place the pan on it. Place the Crisp Lid on top of the inner pot and plug it in.

3. Cook at 330°F for 15 minutes, check that the frittata is set by inserting the centre with a toothpick. Frittata is ready when the inserted toothpick emerges clean.

4. Remove pan carefully and serve hot.

Nutritional Information Per Serving

Calories - 141, Carbohydrates – 2g, Fat – 10g, Proteins – 8g, Fiber – g

Air Fried Breakfast Sausage

Prep Time: 5 minutes

Cook Time: 10 minutes

Servings: 2

Ingredients

2 sausage links

½ teaspoon of celery salt

½ teaspoon of garlic powder

1 small egg

Instructions

1. Begin by chopping the sausages into mince.

2. To the minced sausage; add the egg, celery salt and garlic powder. Form into 2 patties and place in the fryer basket.

3. Set the Crisp lid trivet in the inner pot of your pressure cooker, place the fryer basket on top and set the Crisp lid on top of the inner pot. Plug in.

4. Set the temperature to 350°F and cook for 10 minutes. Remove and serve.

Nutritional Information Per Serving

Calories - 163, Carbohydrates –3g, Fat – 9g, Proteins –17g, Cholesterol: 118mg

Baked Egg Cups With Spinach & Cheese

Delicious, super quick and simple!

Prep Time: 5 minutes

Cook Time: 10minutes

Servings: 2

Ingredients

2 large eggs

2 tablespoons milk or half & half

2 tablespoons frozen spinach, thawed

2 teaspoons grated cheese

Salt & black pepper, to taste

Cooking Spray

Instructions

1. Spray muffin cups or ramekin with cook spray. Add in the egg, milk, cheese, spinach and cheese. Add salt and pepper to season and stir gently without breaking the egg yolks.

2. Place in the fryer basket. Place the pressure cooker trivet in the inner steel pot. Place the basket of ramekins on the trivet. Place the Crisp Lid on top of the inner pot and plug it in. Set to 330°F for 10 minutes, checking every 5 minutes.

3. Cook egg to desired texture.

Nutritional Information Per Serving

Calories - 86, Carbohydrates –2g, Fat – 5g, Proteins –7g, Cholesterol: 188mg, Fiber: 0g

Egg And Cheese Scramble

Flavor rich and texture -prefect breakfast meal to make your morning,

Prep Time: 5 minutes

Cook Time: 3 minutes

Servings: 2

Ingredients

4 large eggs, beaten

1/2 tablespoon of cream cheese

2 tablespoons of grated cheddar cheese

Salt and pepper

Instructions

1. Add the cream cheese and beaten eggs in a bowl, together with a little salt and pepper and whisk to combine all.

2. Spritz pan with cooking spray. Place the trivet in the pot and then place the pan on it. Place the Crisp Lid on top of the inner pot and plug it in.

3. Set to 320°F and cook 2 minutes. Stir in the eggs with a spatula and once the eggs are almost cooked, add the cheese and cook another minute.

4. Remove to a dish and serve with sausage or bacon.

Nutritional Information Per Serving

Calories - 255, Carbohydrates – 2.52g, Fat – 16.69g, Proteins – 15.13g, Fiber – g

PORK

Air Fryer Pork Loin

A healthy meal under 30 minutes!

Prep Time: 2 minutes

Cook Time: 20 minutes

Servings: 2

Ingredients

8 oz. pork tenderloin

Cooking spray

1 small roasted garlic

Salt & pepper

Instructions

1. Pat dry tenderloin and coat with cooking spray. Sprinkle with salt and pepper and rub with roasted garlic. Place in the basket.

2. Set the Crisp lid trivet in the inner pot of your pressure cooker, place the fryer basket on top and set the Crisp lid on top of the inner pot. Plug in.

3. Cook at 400°F for 10 minutes on one side. Flip and cook another 10 minutes. Cool for 5 minutes and enjoy!

Nutritional Information Per Serving

Calories - 379, Fat – 10g, Proteins – 62g, Cholesterol: 196mg

BBQ Pork Chops

Prep Time: 10 minutes

Cook Time: 25 minutes

Servings: 2-3

Ingredients

13 oz. (6 small pieces) fresh pork loin, (roasts), boneless

1 cup barbecue sauce

10 rings onions, raw

Cook spray

2 tablespoons of parmesan cheese, grated

1 teaspoon of garlic powder

Instructions

1. Place the onions in the fryer basket, spray with cooking spray. Set the Crisp lid trivet in the inner pot of your pressure cooker, place the fryer basket on top and set the Crisp lid on top of the inner pot. Plug in.

2. Cook at 360°F for 10 minutes until golden. Remove to a plate. Add the meat and sprinkle the cheese and garlic powder over it. Spread the BBQ sauce on top.

3. Cook 425°F for 10 minutes. Flip and cook at 400°F for 5 more minutes. Cool, combine with the golden onion rings and enjoy!

Nutritional Information Per Serving

Calories - 321, Carbohydrates – 5.7g Fat – 14.7g, Proteins – 39g, Fiber: 0.76g

Vietnamese Pork Noodle

Make this "Bun Thit Nuong" crispier in an air fryer. A Vietnamese dish of pork, noodles, fresh herbs and nut. You'll love it, the Crisp Lid way!

Prep Time: 40 minutes

Cook Time: 15 minutes

Servings: 2

Ingredients

1/8 cup of minced onions

1 tablespoon olive oil

1/2 tablespoon erythritol

1 teaspoon of dark soy sauce

1/2 tablespoon garlic, minced

Handful fresh lemongrass, minced

½ tablespoon fish sauce

½/ teaspoon ground black pepper

½ pound pork shoulder, thinly sliced

For Finishing

1/8 cup roasted peanuts, crushed

1 tablespoons cilantro or parsley, chopped

Instructions

1. Combine in a bowl; the onions, sweetener, oil, soy sauce, fish sauce, lemongrass, garlic and pepper.

2. Slice the pork shoulder thinly into 1/2 inch slices, cut again diagonally into 4-inch pieces. Place in the marinade for 30 minutes to 24 hours. Place in the refrigerator.

3. Transfer marinated pork to the fryer basket, Place trivet in pot. Place basket on it. Set the Crisp Lid on the inner steel pot of the pressure cooker and plug in.

4. Cook at 400°F for 15 minutes, flipping over halfway. Remove when inserted meat thermometer reads at least 165°F.

5. Serve, sprinkled with roasted nuts and parsley. Enjoy with cooked noodles.

Nutritional Information Per Serving

Calories - 231, Carbohydrates – 4g Fat – 16g, Proteins – 16g, Fiber: 1g

Breaded Pork Chops

Breaded Pork Chops

Prep Time: 15 minutes

Cook Time: 15 minutes

Servings: 2

Ingredients

1 cup of pork rinds

1/2 teaspoon freshly ground black pepper

1/2 teaspoon kosher salt

1/2 teaspoon dried oregano

1/2 teaspoon dried parsley flakes

1/2 teaspoon garlic powder

1/4 teaspoon dried basil

1/4 cup spicy brown mustard

1/4 teaspoon onion powder

2 1-inch thick pork chops

Instructions

1. Smash the pork rinds, add to a bowl. Add the seasoning and mix to combine well.

2. Spread the mustard on the pork chops on both sides and ensure it coats well with the pork rind coating.

3. Spray fryer basket, place in the chops. Set the Crisp lid trivet in the inner pot of your pressure cooker, place the fryer basket on top and set the Crisp lid on top of the inner pot. Plug in.

4. Cook for 350°F for 15 minutes, flipping halfway.

Nutritional Information Per Serving

Calories - 209, Carbohydrates – 2g, Fat – 11g, Proteins – 20g, Fiber – 2g, Cholesterol: 27mg

Parmesan Crusted Pork Chops

Prep Time: 5 minutes

Cook Time: 15 minutes

Servings: 2

Ingredients

2 thick center cut pork chops, boneless

1/4 teaspoon salt

Pinch teaspoon pepper

¼ teaspoon onion powder

½ teaspoon smoked paprika

Pinch teaspoon chili powder

1egg beaten

½ cup pork rind crumbs

11/2 tbsp. grated parmesan cheese

Instructions

1. Season the pork chops with the salt and pepper.

2. Blend the pork rinds into crumbs. Use a food processor for this.

3. In a large bowl, add together the crumbs and the seasonings. With the beaten eggs in a separate bowl, dip the pork chops, one after the other in the egg bowl and then the crumb mix.

4. Transfer to fryer basket. Set the Crisp lid trivet in the inner pot of your pressure cooker, place the fryer basket on top and set the Crisp lid on top of the inner pot. Plug in.

5. Cook at 400°F for 15 minutes.

Nutritional Information Per Serving

Calories - 717, Carbohydrates – 3g, Fat – 36g, Proteins – 91g, Fiber – 8g, Cholesterol: 285mg

BEEF

Salisbury Steak Burgers

A quick meal prep delight!

Prep Time: 2 minutes

Cook Time: 15 minutes

Servings: 2

Ingredients

1 lb. of minced beef

½ small onion, sliced thinly

3 large garlic cloves, sliced thinly

1 teaspoon of tomato paste

3 teaspoon paprika

2 teaspoon mustard powder

Salt & Pepper

Pinch Cayenne pepper

Instructions

1. Add together all ingredients in a bowl and form into burgers.

2. Place in the fryer basket. Set the Crisp lid trivet in the inner pot of your pressure cooker, place the fryer basket on top and set the Crisp lid on top of the inner pot. Plug in.

3. Cook at 320°F for 15 minutes. Serve.

Nutritional Information Per Serving

Calories - 674, Carbohydrates – 7g, Fat – 51g, Proteins – 44g, Fiber – 1g, Cholesterol: 177mg

Air Fryer Hamburgers

Prep time: 15minutes

Cook time: 20 minutes

Servings: 2

Ingredients

2 strips bacon, thinly cut

2 (4-oz) hamburger patties, ½ inch thick

½ teaspoon kosher salt

¼ teaspoon garlic powder

¼ teaspoon onion powder

¼ teaspoon smoky paprika

¼ teaspoon fresh ground pepper

Optional Toppings:

2 (1-oz) sharp cheddar cheese slice

1 slice red onion

2 slices tomato

¼ avocado, sliced

2 large butter lettuce leaves

Instructions

1. Place the bacon in the fryer basket. Place trivet in pot. Place basket on it. Set the Crisp Lid on the inner steel pot of the pressure cooker and plug in. Cook at 375°F for 5 minutes.

2. While it cooks, combine in a small bowl, the garlic powder, onion powder, paprika, pepper, and salt and stir to mix.

3. Remove bacon, place on a plate lined with paper towel and set aside.

4. Season the patties generously with seasoning mixture and place in the basket. Return Crisp Lid and cook for 10 minutes at 375°F. Open and add the cheese slices and cook to melt for about a minute

4. Remove burgers, serve with optional toppings, and Ranch dressing or mustard.

Nutritional Information Per Serving

Calories - 521, Carbohydrates – 6g, Fat – 42g, Proteins – 32g, Fiber – 3g

Super Easy Steak

Cook steaks over 1-inch thick for 10 minutes or more. If 2 inches thick, cook 20 minutes and if an inch thick, cook 5 minutes.

Prep Time: 5minutes

Cook Time: 10minutes

Servings: 2

Ingredients

2 (8 oz) ribeye steaks, boneless

1 tablespoon steak seasoning of choice

1 tablespoon unsalted butter

1 teaspoon kosher salt

Instructions

1. Rub the steaks with the seasoning and salt. Let it rest for about 30 minutes to marinate well.

2. Place the steaks in the fryer basket in a single layer, and set the trivet in the pot of the pressure cooker. Place the fryer basket on the trivet and then set the Crisp lid on the pot and plug it in.

3. Set temperature to 500°F and cook for 5 minutes; flip and cook again for 5 minutes. Transfer to a cutting board and add 1½ teaspoons of butter to each of the steak. Let it rest 5-7 minutes and then slice.

4. Enjoy with greens of choice along with boiled rice.

Nutritional Information Per Serving

Calories - 176, Carbohydrates – 2g, Fat – 14g, Proteins – 11g,

Keto Meatloaf Sliders

Prep time: 30 minutes

Cook time: 15 minutes

Servings: 2

Ingredients

4 oz. ground beef

1 small eggs, beaten

1 tablespoon of finely chopped onion

½ clove garlic, minced

1 tablespoon of blanched almond flour

1 tablespoon of coconut flour

1 tablespoon of ketchup

Pinch kosher salt & Pinch black pepper

1/4 teaspoon Italian Seasoning

1/4 tablespoons of Worcestershire Sauce

Pinch Tarragon, dried

Instructions

1. Add together all the ingredients, mix and make even patties. Refrigerate for 15 minutes to harden.

2. Place in the fryer basket. Place trivet in pot. Place basket on it. Set the Crisp Lid on the inner steel pot of the pressure cooker and plug in.

3. Cook at 360°F for 15 minutes. Enjoy with some spring greens.

Nutritional Information Per Serving

Calories - 485, Carbohydrates – 7g, Fat – 28g, Proteins – 51g, Fiber – 2g, Cholesterol: 233mg

Beef Kheema Meatloaf

Enjoy meatloaf the Indian way!

Prep Time: 10 minutes

Cook Time: 20 minutes

Servings: 2

Ingredients

8 oz. lean ground beef

1 eggs

½ cup onion diced

1/8 cup chopped cilantro

½ tablespoon minced garlic

½ tablespoon minced ginger

½ teaspoon salt

1 teaspoon garam masala

½ teaspoon turmeric

½ teaspoon cayenne

1/4 teaspoon ground cinnamon

Pinch ground cardamom

Instructions

1. Add all ingredients in a bowl, mix thoroughly to season meat.

2. Transfer meat to a round pan.

3. Set the Crisp lid trivet in the inner pot of your pressure cooker, place the pan on top and set the Crisp lid on top of the inner pot. Plug in.

4. Cook at 375°F for 15 minutes. Remove, once an internal temperature of 160°F is attained. Drain excess liquid. *Serve!*

Nutritional Information Per Serving

Calories - 190, Carbohydrates – 7g, Fat – 10g, Proteins – 25g, Fiber – 1g, Cholesterol: 153mg

Juicy Crispy Steak

The best juicy air fryer steak that's cooked to perfection!

Prep Time: 5 minutes

Cook Time: 20 minutes

Servings: 2

Ingredients

2 medium size rib eye steaks

Salt and pepper

Instructions

1. Wash the steaks, dry with paper towel and sprinkle with salt and pepper.

2. Place in the fryer basket. Set the Crisp lid trivet in the inner pot of your pressure cooker, place the fryer basket on top and set the Crisp lid on top of the inner pot. Plug in.

3. Cook at 400°F for 20 minutes, flipping half way.

Nutritional Information Per Serving

Calories - 470, Fat – 31g, Proteins – 45g, Cholesterol: 137mg

POULTRY

Pop Almond Chicken

Deliciously keto!

Prep Time: 15minutes

Cook Time: 15minutes

Servings: 2

Ingredients

1 lb. skinless chicken tenders

½ cup Glucomannan powder

1 cup lite culinary coconut milk

1 teaspoon pickle juice

3 cups of almond flakes, crushed finely

½ teaspoon onion powder

½ teaspoon garlic powder

¼ teaspoon black pepper

½ teaspoon paprika

¼ teaspoon cayenne pepper (optional)

Instructions

1. Cut the chicken into cubes. Put the Glucomannan powder in a plate. Add the pickle juice and coconut milk together in a bowl. Add the almond flakes, along with the spices in plastic bag and crush. Place crushed flakes in a separate plate.

2. Now dip a chicken cube in the Glucomannan powder, dip in the coconut milk and roll cubes in the flakes. Repeat for all chicken pieces.

3. Add rolled chicken cubes to fryer basket, working in batches. Set the Crisp lid trivet in the inner pot of your pressure cooker, place the fryer basket on top and set the Crisp lid on top of the inner pot. Plug in.

4. Cook at 400°F for 15 minutes on, checking and tossing halfway through.

Nutritional Information Per Serving

Calories - 417, Carbohydrates – 6g, Fat – 22g, Proteins – 20g, Fiber –64g; Cholesterol 32 mg

Keto Crisp Chicken
Crispy with the perfect grain-free breading!

Prep Time: 10 minutes

Cook Time: 20 minutes

Servings: 2-3

Ingredients

3/4 lbs. chicken drumsticks

1/8 cup of coconut flour

1/4 teaspoon of kosher salt

1/8 teaspoon of black pepper

1 large egg

½ cup pork rinds, crushed

½ teaspoon of smoked paprika

1/8 teaspoon of dried thyme

1/4 teaspoon of garlic powder

Instructions

1. Combine in a shallow bowl; the coconut flour, salt and black pepper.

2. In a separate bowl, whisk the eggs together. In a third bowl, combine the pork rinds, together with the smoked paprika, the garlic powder and the thyme.

3. First dredge the pieces inside the coconut flour mix, dip in the eggs and then shake excess off. Next, press the chicken pieces into the pork rind mix.

4. Arrange in the fryer basket in a single layer. Spray cooking spray over basket. Place trivet in pressure cooker inner steel pot and place the basket on trivet.

5. Place the Crisp Lid on top of the inner pot and plug it in. Set to 400°F for 20 minutes until it attains an internal temperature of 165°F.

Nutritional Information Per Serving

Calories - 463, Carbohydrates – 3g, Fat – 27g, Proteins – 52g, Fiber – 7g

Baked Chicken Nuggets

Enjoy a healthy, gluten free, weeknight dinner!

Prep Time: 15minutes

Cook Time: 15 minutes

Servings: 2-3

Ingredients

8 oz. boneless, skinless chicken breast, diced

Pinch sea salt

½ tsp. sesame oil

2 tablespoons of coconut flour

1/2 tsp. ground ginger

2 egg whites

3 tablespoons of toasted sesame seeds

Cooking spray

For The Dip:

1 tablespoon of natural creamy almond butter

2 teaspoon of Coconut aminos or gluten-free soy sauce

1/2 tablespoon of water

1 teaspoon of rice vinegar

Sriracha, to taste

1/4 teaspoon of ground ginger

1/4 teaspoon of Monkfruit

Instructions

1. Place the chicken nuggets in a bowl, toss with salt and sesame oil.

2. In a large Ziploc bag, place the coconut flour and the ground ginger. Shake and then add the chicken to coat.

3. Spray fryer basket with cook spray and then arrange the nuggets in them.

4. Set the Crisp lid trivet in the inner pot of your pressure cooker, place the fryer basket on top and set the Crisp lid on top of the inner pot. Plug in.

5. Cook for 400°F for 10 minutes, flipping halfway; cook until crispy.

6. Meanwhile, combine all the sauce ingredients in a bowl and mix until smooth.

7. Serve nuggets, dipped in sauce.

Nutritional Information Per Serving

Calories - 286, Carbohydrates – 10g, Fat – 11g, Proteins – 29g, Fiber – 5g

Chicken Wings With Buffalo Sauce

Prep Time: 20 minutes

Cook Time: 30 minutes

Servings: 2-3

Ingredients

For the wings:

1 lb. chicken wingettes

Cooking spray

¼ teaspoon garlic powder

1/4 teaspoon salt

Extra oil for greasing

Buffalo Sauce:

¼ cup hot pepper sauce

1/8 cup coconut oil

½ tablespoon of white vinegar

Ground cayenne pepper to taste

Instructions

1. Spray chicken wings with oil and then sprinkle over with salt and garlic powder.

2. Spray fryer basket with cooking spray and then lay the wings on it in an even layer.

3. Set the Crisp lid trivet in the inner pot of your pressure cooker, place the fryer basket on top and set the Crisp lid on top of the inner pot. Plug in.

4. Cook at 360°F for 25 minutes. Flip and cook at 400°F for 5 minutes.

5. Meanwhile, in a small pot, add together the hot sauce, vinegar, butter and ground pepper and then bring to a boil. Whisk, remove and set aside.

6. Add cooked wings to sauce and coat evenly. Serve with desired dressing and celery.

Nutritional Information Per Serving

Calories - 327, Carbohydrates – 0g, Fat – 27g, Proteins – 18g, Cholesterol: 99mg

Asian Barbecue Satay

Prep Time: 15 minutes

Cook Time: 15 minutes

Servings: 2-3

Ingredients

4 garlic cloves, chopped

¾ pound (12 oz.) chicken tenders, boneless & skinless

½ cup pineapple juice

½ cup soy sauce

¼ cup of sesame oil

4 scallions, chopped

2 teaspoons sesame seeds, toasted

1 tablespoon fresh ginger, grated

Pinch black pepper

Instructions

1. Skewer the chicken tender, trimming excess fat.

2. Combine remaining ingredients in a bowl. Add the skewered chicken to it. Combine well, cover and chill 2 to 24hours.

3. Pat dry chicken. Add the skewers to the basket. Set the Crisp lid trivet in the inner pot of your pressure cooker, place the fryer basket on top and set the Crisp lid on top of the inner pot. Plug in.

4. Cook at 390°F for 10 minutes on both sides.

Nutritional Information Per Serving

Calories - 277, Carbohydrates – 14g, Fat – 20g, Proteins – 12g, Fiber- 2g Cholesterol: 16mg

Crispy Garlic Ranch Wings

Well- marinated chicken wings prepared in the Crisp Lid. You won't want to miss this!

Prep Time: 20 minutes

Cook Time: 25 minutes

Servings: 2

Ingredients

1 1/2 tablespoons of Ranch Seasoning Mix

1/8 cup of melted butter

3 cloves of minced garlic

1 pound chicken wings

Instructions

1. Combine marinade ingredients. Place wings in a Ziploc bag, pour in the marinade and shake up to coat. Let it marinate in the refrigerator for 4 hours or overnight.

2. Place in the fryer basket. Set the Crisp lid trivet in the inner pot of your pressure cooker, place the fryer basket on top and set the Crisp lid on top of the inner pot. Plug in.

3. Cook at 360°F for 20 minutes, shaking every 10 minutes. Afterwards increase the temperature to 400°F and cook another 5 minutes.

Nutritional Information Per Serving

Calories - 411, Carbohydrates – 7g, Fat – 31g, Proteins – 22g, – Cholesterol: 124mg

Turkish Chicken Bites

Prep Time: 45 minutes

Cook Time: 15 minutes

Servings: 2

Ingredients

1/8 cup of plain Greek yogurt

½ tablespoon of garlic, minced

½ tablespoon of tomato paste

½ tablespoon of coconut oil

½ tablespoon of lemon juice

½ teaspoon of salt

½ teaspoon of smoked paprika

½ teaspoon of ground cumin

¼ teaspoon of ground black pepper

¼ teaspoon of ground cinnamon

¼ teaspoon of cayenne

8 oz. chicken thighs, boneless skinless, cut into 2 pieces

Instructions

1. Combine all the spice ingredients in a large bowl: the Greek yogurt, lemon juice, garlic, the tomato paste, oil, salt, cinnamon, paprika, black pepper, cumin, and the cayenne pepper

2. Now add the chicken and mix to coat well with the marinade. Let it stay for 30 minutes in the refrigerator or if possible, 12-24 hours.

3. Remove chicken, place in the fryer basket, set the Crisp lid trivet in the inner pot of your pressure cooker, place the basket on top and set the Crisp lid on top of the inner pot. Plug in.

4. Cook at 375°F for 10 minutes. Remove the Crisp Lid, set on silicon trivet, flip and cook 5 more minutes. Remove once an inserted meat thermometer reads 150°F.

5. Serve!

Nutritional Information Per Serving

Calories - 298, Carbohydrates – 4g, Fat – 23g, Proteins – 20g, – Cholesterol: 112mg, Fiber: 1g

Crispy Sausage Dinner
A weeknight favorite!

Prep Time: 5 minutes

Cook Time: 12 minutes

Servings: 2

Ingredients

2 Chicken Sausages

Cooking Spray

Instructions

1. Spray basket. Place sausages in.

2. Place the trivet in the inner pot of pressure cooker. Place basket on trivet. Set the Crisp Lid on the pot and plug it in. Set temperature to cook at 350°F for 12 minutes, tossing halfway through.

Nutritional Information Per Serving

Calories - 238, Carbohydrates – 1g, Fat – 14g, Proteins – 25g, – Cholesterol: 119mg, Fiber: 0g

Tandoori Chicken

Full of flavor, and easy to make, you will find this chicken tandoori, with its rich yoghurt marinade, a delight.

Prep Time: 30 minutes

Cook Time: 20 minutes

Servings: 2

Ingredients

8 oz. chicken tenders, halved

¼ cup Greek yogurt

½ tablespoon garlic, minced

½ tablespoon ginger, minced

1/8 cup cilantro

½ teaspoon salt

¼ teaspoon cayenne

½ teaspoon turmeric

½ teaspoon smoked paprika

½ teaspoon garam masala

½ tablespoon ghee, to baste

1 teaspoon lemon juice, to finish

1 tablespoon chopped cilantro, to garnish

Instructions

1. Combine all the ingredients in a bowl, but set aside 2 tablespoons of cilantro, basting oil and lemon juice.

2. Place the chicken, (in batches) in the fryer, baste with ghee on one side. Set the Crisp lid trivet in the inner pot of your pressure cooker, place the fryer basket on top and set the Crisp lid on top of the inner pot. Plug in.

3. Cook at 350°F for 15 minutes. Flip, baste with ghee and cook 5 more minutes. Remove when meat thermometer reads 165°F.

4. Serve on a plate. Add lemon juice, mix, and sprinkle with cilantro. Serve with naan.

Nutritional Information Per Serving

Calories - 178, Carbohydrates – 2g, Fat – 6g, Proteins – 25g

Buffalo Chicken Meatballs

Prep Time: 15 minutes

Cook Time: 30 minutes

Servings: 2-3

Ingredients

3/4 lb. ground chicken

1/3 cup almond meal

1/2 teaspoon of sea salt

1 garlic cloves, minced

1 green onions, thinly sliced

1 tablespoons of ghee

3 tablespoons of hot sauce

Cooking spray

Chopped green onions, for garnish

Instructions

1. Add together the chicken, almond meal, garlic cloves, green onions and salt in a large bowl and combine thoroughly with your hands.

2. Grease hands with coconut oil and shape into 1-2 inches wide meatballs. Add to basket. Spray with cooking spray.

3. Set the Crisp lid trivet in the inner pot of your pressure cooker, place the fryer basket on top and set the Crisp lid on top of the inner pot. Plug in.

4. Cook at 400°F for 15 minutes until browned. Open the Crisp Lid and add the hot sauce on top of the browned meatballs. Spritz with cooking spray.

5. Cook at 400°F for 15 minutes. Enjoy with cauliflower rice.

Nutritional Information Per Serving

Calories - 357, Carbohydrates – 3g, Fat – 28g, Proteins – 23g, – Fiber: 1 g

Keto Drumsticks

Cook a healthy chicken drumstick meal in your Crisp Lid. It is so easy!

Prep Time: 5minutes

Cook Time: 25minutes

Servings: 2

Ingredients

4 drumsticks chicken, skin on

Cooking spray

1 teaspoon paprika

1/2 teaspoon garlic powder

1/2 teaspoon onion powder

1/2 teaspoon turmeric

1 teaspoon salt

1/2 teaspoon black pepper

Instructions

1. Add all the dry seasonings together in a small bowl.

2. Rub drumstick with the oil and seasonings to coat evenly.

3. Place in the fryer basket in an even layer. Set the Crisp lid trivet in the inner pot of your pressure cooker, place the fryer basket on top and set the Crisp lid on top of the inner pot. Plug in.

4. Cook at 400°F for 12 minutes. Flip halfway and cook another 12 or 13 minutes. Let it cook and enjoy with preferred veggies.

Nutritional Information Per Serving

Calories - 171, Carbohydrates – 2g, Fat – 8g, Proteins – 22g, Fiber – 1g

Chicken Coconut Meatballs
Simple melt- in- your- mouth meatballs that's flavorful and different!

Prep Time: 10 minutes

Cook Time: 15 minutes

Servings: 2

Ingredients

8 oz. ground chicken

1 green onions, finely chopped

1/4 cup cilantro, chopped

1/2 tablespoon hoisin sauce

½ tablespoon soy sauce

½ teaspoon sriracha sauce

Cooking oil spray

1/8 cup unsweetened shredded coconut

Salt & ground black pepper to taste to taste

Instructions

1. Combine all the ingredients in a bowl.

2. Shape into meatballs. Add to basket. Spray with cooking spray.

3. Set the Crisp lid trivet in the inner pot of your pressure cooker, place the fryer basket on top and set the Crisp lid on top of the inner pot. Plug in.

4. Cook at 400°F for 15 minutes, flipping once until an internal temperature of 150 to 165F is attained.

Nutritional Information Per Serving

Calories - 233, Carbohydrates – 3g, Fat – 14g, Proteins – 20g, Fiber – 1g

Brazilian Chicken
Prep Time: 5 minutes

Cook Time: 25 minutes

Servings: 2

Ingredients

½ teaspoon dried oregano

½ teaspoon cumin seeds

½ teaspoon dried parsley

½ teaspoon kosher salt

½ teaspoon turmeric

1/4 teaspoon whole black peppercorns

1/4 teaspoon coriander seeds

1/4 teaspoon cayenne

1/8 cup lime juice

Cooking spray

¾ lb. chicken drumsticks

Instructions

1. Blend together all the spices in a coffee grinder.

2. Transfer to a medium bowl and then add the lime juice and cooking spray. Add the chicken drumsticks and coat with marinade. Let it remain marinated in the refrigerator for several hours.

3. Place in the fryer basket, (work in batches) with the skin side up. Set the Crisp lid trivet in the inner pot of your pressure cooker, place the basket on top and set the Crisp lid on top of the inner pot. Plug in.

4. Cook at 400°F for 25 minutes, flipping halfway. Check for doneness at 165F.

Nutritional Information Per Serving

Calories - 253, Carbohydrates – 2g, Fat – 17g, Proteins – 20g

Crispy Chicken Nuggets

Prep Time: 10 minutes

Cook Time: 20 minutes

Servings: 2

Ingredients

8 oz. chicken tenders

½ bag pork rinds

1/4 cup parmesan cheese

½ teaspoon garlic powder

½ teaspoon paprika

1/8 cup mayo

Instructions

1. Crush pork rinds and pour in a shallow bowl. Add the cheese and spices and mix to incorporate.

2. Cut the tenders in a bowl and add the mayonnaise on top. Move the chicken around to coat with the mayo.

3. Dredge chicken with pork rinds and place in the fryer basket.

4. Cook at 400°F for 15- 20 minutes. Serve immediately.

Nutritional Information Per Serving

Calories - 490, Carbohydrates – 3g, Fat – 29g, Proteins – 53g, Fiber – 6g

Butter Chicken With Broccoli

Enjoy a quick tasty dinner of fried chicken and hearty broccoli.

Prep Time: 5 minutes

Cook Time: 15 minutes

Servings: 2

Ingredients

3½ oz. butter

8- 10 oz. boneless chicken thighs

1 cup broccoli, rinsed, trimmed & cut

Salt and pepper

½ cup mayonnaise, optional

Instructions

1. Coat the chicken with the salt and pepper, transfer to fryer basket and then place butter on top.

2. Set the Crisp lid trivet in the inner pot of your pressure cooker, place the basket on top and set the Crisp lid on top of the inner pot. Plug in.

3. Cook at 400°F for 15 minutes, flipping halfway.

4. Remove Crisp Lid, place on silicon trivet, add the rinsed, trimmed and cut pieces of broccoli, cover and cook at 350°F for 5 minutes.

5. Remove chicken and broccoli and enjoy!

Nutritional Information Per Serving

Calories - 733, Carbohydrates – 5g, Fat – 66g, Proteins – 29g

Whole Roast Chicken

This keto-friendly, paleo-friendly, healthy main dish recipe is so easy to make and ready within an hour!

Prep Time: 10 minutes

Cook Time: 1 hr. 10minutes

Servings: 2-4

Ingredients

1 whole chicken (3 lb.)

1 tablespoon canola oil

1/4 teaspoon ground black pepper

1 teaspoon kosher salt

1 lemon, cut into 4

4 cloves garlic

Instructions

1. Place the pressure cooker trivet in the inner pot, in the higher position (with trivet handles up).

2. Rinse the chicken, and then remove the giblets. Pat it dry and then rub with oil all over and season with the salt and pepper. Stuff the cloves and lemon in the cavity of the chicken.

3. Place on the trivet in the inner pot with the breast side down and the legs and wings tucked under the chicken.

4. Set the Crisp Lid on the pot and plug it in. Set temperature to cook at a temperature of 400°F for 40 minutes.

5. Remove Crisp lid and chicken as well, by lifting the handles of the trivet. Flip with tongs and then lower chicken and trivet carefully back to pot, with the trivet handles.

6. Cook until a meat thermometer inserted reads at least 165°F. This should take another 30 to 40 minutes at the same temperature.

7. Cool 5 minutes, carve and enjoy!

Nutritional Information Per Serving

Calories - 338, Carbohydrates –5g, Fat – 10g, Proteins –66g, Cholesterol: 150mg

Keto Air Fried Chicken

A crispy and crunchy chicken made "breaded" in almond flour and parmesan cheese.

Prep Time: 15 minutes

Cook Time: 10 minutes

Servings: 2

Ingredients

2 (about 9 oz. total) boneless skinless chicken thighs

Egg Wash:

1 large eggs

1 tablespoon of heavy whipping cream

For "Breading":

1/3 cup of blanched almond flour

1/3 cup parmesan cheese, finely grated

½ teaspoon of salt

¼ teaspoon of black pepper

1/4 teaspoon cayenne

1/4 teaspoon paprika

Instructions

1. Beat the eggs and heavy cream in a bowl until well-mixed. In a separate bowl, add all the breading together and whisk to mix well. Set aside.

2. Cut chicken thigh into 3 even pieces and pat dry with paper towels.

3. Coat each chicken piece first in the breading, and then in the egg wash, and finally in the breading again, ensuring all sides are well- coated. Shake off excess coating and place in the fryer basket. Spray with cooking spray.

4. Set the Crisp lid trivet in the inner pot of your pressure cooker, place the fryer basket on top and set the Crisp lid on top of the inner pot. Plug in.

5. Cook at 390°F. Set time to 20 minutes, flip halfway during cooking. Serve hot and crispy.

Nutritional Information Per Serving

Calories - 486, Carbohydrates –5g, Fat – 25g, Proteins – 60g, Fiber – 2g, Cholesterol: 331mg

Keto Adobo Chicken Thighs

Tasty chicken thighs with crispy, and flavorful adobo seasoning crust!

Prep Time: 5 minutes

Cook Time: 20 minutes

Servings: 2

Ingredients

2 large chicken thighs

1 tablespoon adobo seasoning

Cooking spray

Instructions

1. Spritz chicken with cooking spray and toss in adobo seasoning to coat.

2. Place in fryer basket, Place trivet in pot. Place basket on it. Set the Crisp Lid on the inner steel pot of the pressure cooker and plug in.

3. Cook at 350 F for 10 minutes. Flip and cook an additional for10 minutes. Meat thermometer inserted should read 165F, afterwards remove. Cool and enjoy!

Nutritional Information Per Serving

Calories - 359, Carbohydrates – 1g, Fat – 24g, Proteins – 36g, Fiber – 1g

Air Fried Turkey Breast

Tasty turkey breast ever!

Prep Time: 15 minutes

Cook Time: 35 minutes

Servings: 2-3

Ingredients

½ oz. packaged onion soup mix

1 turkey breast

2 ribs celery, cut largely into chunks

1 onion, cut largely into chunks

1 cup chicken broth

2 tablespoons water

1 tablespoon cornstarch, or more

Instructions

1. Pour the water, chicken broth, onion soup mix, onion chunks and celery in your pressure cooker inner pot.

2. Place the chicken in the pressure cooker basket and place basket in the pot. Seal the pressure lid and cook on high pressure for 20 minutes. Perform a quick release. Remove pressure lid carefully. Remove chicken to a platter. Pour broth to a bowl. Wipe the inner pot dry. Turn off pressure cooker.

3. Brush turkey with oil, season also with salt and pepper. Place in the fryer basket. Set the Crisp lid trivet in the inner pot of your pressure cooker, place the fryer basket on top and set the Crisp lid on top of the inner pot. Plug in.

4. Set temperature to 400°F, and cook to 15 minutes. Once cooked, remove CrisplLid to silicon trivet. Remove basket. Unplug Crisp Lid.

5. Transfer the remaining broth to the inner pot of your pressure cooker. Add water and cornstarch in a bowl; mix and add to the pot. Press the sauté function and whisk 2 -3 minutes until thickened.

6. Serve the gravy and enjoy with crispy turkey.

Nutritional Information Per Serving

Calories - 584, Carbohydrates –5g, Fat – 22g, Proteins – 85.7g,

FISH & SEAFOOD

Salmon Yoghurt Fillets

Fresh or frozen salmon is infused with lemon and cooked in the Crisp Lid for a perfect meal. Enjoy with Greek yogurt garlic sauce for everyone!

Prep Time: 5 minutes

Cook Time: 15 minutes

Servings: 2

Ingredients

2 4 oz. salmon fillets

Salt and freshly ground pepper

1 lemon, sliced

1 tablespoon of fresh dill, chopped

1/4 cup Greek yogurt

1 teaspoon lemon juice

1/2 teaspoon garlic powder

Instructions

1. Begin by washing the fillets and then drying with paper towels.

2. Place the sliced lemon in the fryer basket. Sprinkle the fish with salt and pepper and place on top of the sliced lemon in the basket.

3. Set the Crisp lid trivet in the inner pot of your pressure cooker, place the fryer basket on top and set the Crisp lid on top of the inner pot. Plug in.

4. Cook at a temperature of 330F for 15 minutes.

5. As it cooks, make the sauce by combining the yoghurt, dill and garlic powder in a bowl. Add the lemon juice and if desired, a sprinkle of salt and pepper.

6. Remove cooked salmon and cover with the sauce. *Yummy!*

Nutritional Information Per Serving

Calories - 194, Carbohydrates – 6g, Fat – 29g, Proteins – 25g, Fiber – 1g

Crispy Breaded Fish Sticks
Simple and sure to please!

Prep Time: 5 minutes

Cook Time: 10 minutes

Servings: 2

Ingredients

8 oz. cod or any other white fish

½ cup of mayonnaise

1 tablespoon Dijon mustard

1 tablespoon water

¾ cups pork rind panko

3/4 teaspoon Cajun seasoning

Salt and pepper to taste

Instructions

1. Pat dry fish and cut.

2. Add together the mustard, mayonnaise and water in a shallow bowl. In another, add together the pork rinds and the Cajun seasoning. Season with salt and pepper.

3. Dip fish in mayo mixture; once coated, shake off and dip into the rind mixture to coat.

4. Spritz fryer basket with avocado oil. Place fish on fryer basket. Place trivet in pot. Place basket on it. Set the Crisp Lid on the inner steel pot of the pressure cooker and plug in.

5. Cook at 400°F for 10 minutes, flipping halfway through. Serve immediately.

Nutritional Information Per Serving

Calories – 263, Carbohydrates – 1g, Fat – 16g, Proteins – 26g, Fiber – 0.5g

Sesame Fish
High- fat and crunchy!

Prep Time: 5minutes

Cook Time: 10minutes

Servings: 2

Ingredients

8 oz. cod

1 tablespoon reduced sodium soy sauce

1 teaspoon honey

Sprinkle of sesame seeds

Instructions

1. Brush the fillets with the soy sauce and honey and then sprinkle with sesame seeds.

2. Place fish on fryer basket. Place trivet in pot. Place basket on it. Set the Crisp Lid on the inner steel pot of the pressure cooker and plug in.

3. Cook at 360F for 10 minutes.

4. Enjoy with cauliflower rice.

Nutritional Information Per Serving

Calories - 128, Carbohydrates – 3g, Fat – 3g, Proteins – 20g, Fiber – 0g

Air-Fried Shrimp Scampi
Simple and delicious!

Prep Time: 5 minutes

Cook Time: 10 minutes

Servings: 2

Ingredients

2 tablespoons butter

1/2 tablespoon lemon juice

½ tablespoon minced garlic

½ tablespoon chopped chives

1 teaspoons red pepper flakes

½ tablespoon minced basil leaves

1 tablespoons chicken Stock

8 oz. shrimp

Instructions

1. Set the Crisp lid trivet in the inner pot of your pressure cooker, place a 6 x 3 pan on top. Add the butter, garlic, and the red pepper flakes to the pan.

2. Set the Crisp lid on top of the inner pot. Plug in. Cook at 330F for 2 minutes, stir once halfway.

3. Remove Crisp Lid, place on silicon trivet and then add the rest of the ingredients gently into the pan and stir.

4. Set the Crisp lid on top of the inner pot. Plug in. Cook at 330F for 5 minutes, mixing well to coat shrimp in buttery spice.

5. Remove pan with silicone mitts, let it rest for 1-2 minutes. Serve, sprinkled with additional fresh basil leaves, if desired.

Nutritional Information Per Serving

Calories - 173, Carbohydrates – 1g, Fat – 12g, Proteins – 28g, Fiber – 0g, Cholesterol: 204mg

Coconut Shrimp

Make a salad and enjoy this coconut crispy shrimp as a weeknight meal.

Prep Time: 15minutes

Cook Time: 25 minutes

Servings: 2

Ingredients

4 oz. large shrimp, peeled and deveined

1 tablespoon of almond flour

1 small egg

1/4 cup flaked coconut, unsweetened

Instructions

1. Add the flour to a bowl; in another, beat in the egg and in a third, add the flaked unsweetened coconut.

2. Dip the shrimp, first in the flour and then in the egg, shake out excess and then press in the coconut bowl to coat shrimp.

3. Place in fryer basket in a single layer (cook in batches, if necessary). Set the Crisp lid trivet in the inner pot of your pressure cooker, place the fryer basket on top and set the Crisp lid on top of the inner pot. Plug in.

4. Cook at 400°F for 10 minutes. Flip shrimp halfway though. Remove when is pink and the coconut is golden brown.

Nutritional Information Per Serving

Calories - 158, Carbohydrates – 4g, Fat – 9g, Proteins – 14g, Fiber – 3g, Cholesterol: 158mg

Cajun Butter Baked Salmon

Cajun butter is simply delicious and when added to salmon and baked in your Crisp Lid, makes a perfect dinner for family and friends.

Prep Time: 15 minutes

Cook Time: 30 minutes

Servings: 2-4

Ingredients

2 lemons, sliced into rounds

1 large salmon fillet

Kosher salt & freshly ground black pepper

4 tbsp butter, melted

2 teaspoons of Cajun seasoning

3 cloves garlic, minced

2 tablespoons of whole-grain mustard

1 teaspoon of thyme leaves, fresh

Pinch of crushed red pepper flakes

Green onions, thinly sliced (for serving)

Instructions

1. Place the lemon rounds in a steel pan, in an even layer. Place the salmon on top and add salt and pepper to season.

2. In a small bowl, add together the melted butter, mustard, garlic, Cajun seasoning, red pepper flakes and thyme and then brush all over the salmon.

3. Place pressure cooker trivet in inner pot and place the pan on the trivet. Set the Crisp lid on the pot and plug it.

5. Set to cook at 350°F for 30 minutes and then toss halfway. Cook until butter mixture has thickened. Serve, garnished with green onions.

Nutritional Information Per Serving

Calories - 98, Carbohydrates – 3g, Fat – 8g, Proteins – 4g, Fiber – 0g, Cholesterol: 25mg

Cajun Shrimp

Cajun Shrimp

Prep Time: 2 minutes

Cook Time: 6 minutes

Servings: 2

Ingredients

1/2 pound shrimp, peeled & deveined

1/4 teaspoon of cayenne pepper

1/4 teaspoon smoked paprika

Pinch salt

1/2 teaspoon old bay seasoning

Instructions

1. Combine all ingredients in a bowl and mix thoroughly to coat shrimp.

2. Place in the fryer basket. Set the Crisp lid trivet in the inner pot of your pressure cooker, place the fryer basket on top and set the Crisp lid on top of the inner pot. Plug in.

3. Cook at 390°F for 6 minutes, checking and flipping half way through.

Nutritional Information Per Serving

Calories - 68, Carbohydrates –0g, Fat – 0g, Proteins –28g, Cholesterol: 173mg

VEGETABLES

Thai Shrimp Salad

Crisp and nourishing goodness!

Prep Time: 5 minutes

Cook Time: 10 minutes

Servings: 2

Ingredients

6 large shrimps

Juice of 1 small lime

1 tablespoons of red curry paste

½ small cucumber, chopped

½ cup of red cabbage, shredded

½ cup carrots, grated

Handful cilantro

Salt and pepper to taste

Preparation

1. Add together the shrimps, carrots, cucumbers and cabbage in the fryer basket.

2. Set the Crisp lid trivet in the inner pot of your pressure cooker, place the fryer basket on top and set the Crisp lid on top of the inner pot. Plug in. Cook 5-10 minutes at 360°F.

3. Add the remaining ingredients, toss and serve.

Tomato Basil Scallops

An elegant dish of tomatoes, basil, spinach, cream and scallops.

Prep Time: 5 minutes

Cook Time: 10 minutes

Servings: 2

Ingredients

1 12 oz package spinach, frozen, thawed & drained

A sprinkle of salt and pepper

3/4 cup heavy whipping cream

1 tablespoon tomato paste

1 tablespoon fresh basil, chopped

1 teaspoon minced garlic

1/2 teaspoon ground black pepper

1/2 teaspoon salt

8 jumbo sea scallops

Cooking spray

Instructions

1. Spray 6 inch pan with cooking spray and place spinach on it. Spray with oil. Sprinkle with a little salt and pepper, and place the scallops on top of the spinach on the pan.

2. Combine the cream, basil, tomato paste, garlic, salt and pepper in a bowl and pour mixture over the spinach and scallops.

3. Place trivet in pot. Place pan on it. Set the Crisp Lid on the inner steel pot of the pressure cooker and plug in.

4. Cook at 350°F for 10 minutes. Once internal temperature is 135F, remove and serve hot and bubbling.

Nutritional Information Per Serving

Calories - 359, Carbohydrates –6g, Fat – 33g, Proteins – 9g, Fiber –1g

Spinach

Creamed Spinach

The perfect side dish for any entree!

Prep Time: 10 minutes

Cook Time: 15 minutes

Servings: 2

Ingredients

1 10 oz. frozen spinach, thawed

1/4 cup of onion, chopped

4 oz. cream cheese diced

2 teaspoons minced garlic

1 teaspoon salt

1 teaspoon ground black pepper

1/2 teaspoon ground nutmeg

1/4 cup shredded parmesan cheese

Instructions

1. Add together all the ingredients, except the parmesan cheese in a bowl. Transfer to a greased pan.

2. Set the Crisp lid trivet in the inner pot of your pressure cooker, place the pan on top and set the Crisp lid on top of the inner pot. Plug in.

3. Cook at 350°F for 10 minutes. Remove Crisp Lid, place on silicon trivet and stir so that spinach and cream cheese mixes.

4. Sprinkle the parmesan cheese over it. Cook at 400°F for 5 minutes to melt and browned.

Nutritional Information Per Serving

Calories - 273, Carbohydrates –6g, Fat – 23g, Proteins – 8g, Sugar –3g

Asian Sesame Ginger Broccoli
Its broccoli, it's healthy. It's Asian and it's delicious!

Prep Time: 15 minutes

Cook Time: 15 minutes

Servings: 2

Ingredients

1/2 of a bunch broccoli

1 tablespoons olive oil

1 tablespoon toasted sesame oil

1/2 tablespoon white miso

1 teaspoon minced ginger

1/2 tablespoon chili garlic sauce

1/4 teaspoon kosher salt

1/2 teaspoon black sesame seeds

1/2 teaspoon white sesame seeds

1/2 tablespoon thinly sliced scallions

Instructions

1. Cut the broccoli into florets.

2. Add together the olive oil, sesame oil, chili-garlic sauce, miso, the ginger and the salt in a large bowl and mix thoroughly to combine.

3. Add the broccoli and toss to coat all pieces. Transfer to the fryer basket.

4. Set the Crisp lid trivet in the inner pot of your pressure cooker, place the basket on top and set the Crisp lid on top of the inner pot. Plug in.

5. Cook at 400°F for 15 minutes, tossing halfway through. Remove broccoli once crispy and the edges lightly browned.

6. Serve, sprinkled with sesame seeds and green onions.

Nutritional Information Per Serving

Calories - 163, Carbohydrates –13g, Fat – 12g, Proteins – 5g, Fiber –4g

Crispy Moroccan Chickpeas

Prep Time: 5 minutes

Cook Time: 20 minutes

Servings: 2

Ingredients

1 can (15 ounces) chickpeas, rinsed, drained

1 tablespoons extra virgin olive oil, divided

½ teaspoon kosher salt, plus more for seasoning

1 teaspoons garam masala

1/4 teaspoon garlic powder

½ teaspoon of paprika

1/8 teaspoon of ground mustard powder

Instructions

1. Dry the chickpeas thoroughly and place in a bowl. Add a tablespoon of oil and salt and then toss to coat.

2. Press the sauté function of your pressure cooker. Add the chickpeas and sauté for about 5 minutes until golden brown. Unplug pressure cooker.

3. Combine the chickpeas, the remaining oil and the seasonings and toss. Place in the fryer basket. Place trivet in pot. Place basket on it. Set the Crisp Lid on the inner steel pot of the pressure cooker and plug in.

4. Set temperature for 400°F and cook time for 15 minutes. Toss half way through cooking.

5. Remove and serve immediately.

Nutritional Information Per Serving

Calories - 89, Carbohydrates –5g, Fat – 8g, Proteins – 3g, Fiber –1g

Asparagus Fries With Aioli

Prep Time: 25 minutes

Cook Time: 10 minutes

Servings: 2- 4

Ingredients

16 stalks asparagus, trimmed

1 tablespoons coconut flour

1/4 cup of almond meal

½ teaspoon garlic salt

1/4 teaspoon of ground white pepper

1 teaspoons of water

1 small egg

Cooking spray

Lemon Basil Aioli Sauce:

11/2 tablespoons fresh basil

1 teaspoons lemon juice

½ teaspoon minced garlic

1 egg yolks

1/8teaspoon kosher salt

1/8 cup avocado oil

Instructions

1. Wash the asparagus, and then trim into 6 inches.

2. In a shallow dish, add together the coconut flour, almond meal, garlic salt and pepper. Beat the egg in a separate dish.

3. Dip the asparagus spear in the egg and then in the flour mix, one at a time. Spritz with oil.

4. Set the Crisp lid trivet in the inner pot of your pressure cooker, place the fryer basket on top and set the Crisp lid on top of the inner pot. Plug in.

5. Cook at 400°F for 10 minutes.

6. In the meantime, add the basil, lemon juice, garlic, egg yolk and salt in a food processor and pulse to combine. Gently add the avocado oil and pulse for about a minute. Turn off, scrape sides and blend until smooth and well-combined.

7. Serve the crispy asparagus, drizzled with the dipping sauce. Enjoy!

Nutritional Information Per Serving

Calories - 154, Carbohydrates –5g, Fat – 13g, Proteins –4g, Cholesterol: 93mg

Paneer And Cheese Veg Cutlet

Prep Time: 10 minutes

Cook Time: 15 minutes

Servings: 2-3

Ingredients

2 cups of paneer (Cottage Cheese), grated

1 cup of mozzarella cheese

1 onion, finely chopped

1/2 teaspoon of garlic powder

1/2 teaspoon chat masala

1/2 teaspoon salt

1/2 teaspoon oregano seasoning

1 teaspoon ghee

Instructions

1. Add together in a bowl, all the ingredients and make into desired shapes.

2. Place them in the basket. Set the Crisp lid trivet in the inner pot of your pressure cooker, place the fryer basket on top and set the Crisp lid on top of the inner pot. Plug in.

3. Cook at 360F for 10 minutes. Serve hot with sauce and chutney.

Nutritional Information Per Serving

Calories - 159, Carbohydrates –7g, Fat – 7g, Proteins –17g, Cholesterol: 27mg; Fiber: 2g

APPETIZERS & SNACKS

Crispy Jalapeno Coins

A really crispy ketogenic and gluten-free appetizer!

Prep Time: 15 minutes

Cook Time: 10 minutes

Servings: 2-4

Ingredients

1 jalapeno, sliced & seeded

2 tablespoons of coconut flour

Pinch of onion powder

Pinch of garlic powder

Cajun seasoning, optional

Salt & pepper to taste

1 egg, raw, beaten

Cooking spray

Instructions

1. Combine all the dry ingredients in a bowl and mix thoroughly.

2. Remove excess moisture from jalapeno slices by patting dry with paper towel.

3. Now dip jalapeno in the egg wash and then dip in the dry mixture, coating and ensuring it sticks well.

4. Arrange jalapeno slices in the fryer basket in a single layer. Spray with oil. Set the Crisp lid trivet in the inner pot of your pressure cooker, place the fryer basket on top and set the Crisp lid on top of the inner pot. Plug in.

5. Cook 5 minutes at a temperature of 400°F, flip and cook until crisp. Enjoy hot!

Nutritional Information Per Serving

Calories - 69, Carbohydrates – 5g, Fat – 3g, Proteins – 4g, Fiber – 3g

Bacon Wrapped Asparagus

Prep Time: 5 minutes

Cook Time: 10minutes

Servings: 2

Ingredients

1 bunch fresh asparagus

Olive oil spray

6 slices bacon, uncooked, cut in half

Instructions

1. Wrap a bacon piece around 2 asparagus stalks and spray all the pieces with olive oil and a sprinkle of salt.

2. Place in the fryer basket. Set the Crisp lid trivet in the inner pot of your pressure cooker, place the fryer basket on top and set the Crisp lid on top of the inner pot. Plug in.

3. Cook at 390°F for 10 minutes.

Nutritional Information Per Serving

Calories - 127, Carbohydrates –0g, Fat – 12g, Proteins –4g, Cholesterol: 18mg

Roasted Turnips

A quick and easy creamy appetizer that's taste so good!

Prep Time: 10 minutes

Cook Time: 10 minutes

Servings: 2

Ingredients

2 medium turnips

1 teaspoons avocado oil

3/4 teaspoon paprika

1/2 teaspoon cracked pepper

1/2 teaspoon sea salt

1 teaspoons minced parsley

Instructions

1. Prepare the turnips by peeling and dicing. Place in a bowl.

2. Coat with the rest of the ingredients, except the parsley. Transfer to the fryer basket in an even layer.

3. Set the Crisp lid trivet in the inner pot of your pressure cooker, place the fryer basket on top and set the Crisp lid on top of the inner pot. Plug in.

4. Cook at 450F for 10 minutes. Shake the basket half way. Serve, sprinkled with parsley.

Nutritional Information Per Serving

Calories - 57, Carbohydrates –6, Fat – 4g, Proteins – 1g, Fiber – 2g, Cholesterol: 0mg

Jalapeno Sausage Poppers

Prep Time: 15minutes

Cook Time: 15minutes

Servings: 2

Ingredients

2 Jalapenos

½ cup of cooked & crumbled sausage

1/42 cup shredded cheese

4oz. cream cheese

1 tablespoon sour cream

1/4 cup parmesan cheese

1/4 cup pork rinds

½ teaspoon red pepper flakes

Instructions

1. Cut jalapenos in half, remove the core, scoop out the seeds and then set aside.

2. Add in a medium bowl cheddar cheese, cream cheese, sour cream and sausage together and mix to combine well.

3. Fill the halved jalapeno with the creamy sausage filling.

4. Combine the add pork rinds, the parmesan cheese, and the red pepper flakes in a small bowl.

5. Press the filled jalapenos into the pork rinds mix so that it coats well. Place in the fryer basket.

6. Set the Crisp lid trivet in the inner pot of your pressure cooker, place the fryer basket on top and set the Crisp lid on top of the inner pot. Plug in.

7. Cook at 360F for 10 minutes, flip halfway, spray with cook spray and cook extra 3-5 minutes.

Nutritional Information Per Serving

Calories - 475, Carbohydrates –7g, Fat – 39g, Proteins – 28g, Fiber – 4g, Cholesterol: 110mg

Zucchini Pasta

A very healthy low carb dish, sautéed and then air fried!

Prep Time: 15 minutes

Cook Time: 11 minutes

Servings: 2

Ingredients

4 zucchini, peeled

2 tablespoon avocado oil

1 cup water

Salt and pepper

Instructions

1. Use a vegetable peeler to cut the zucchini into slices lengthwise. Peel until the zucchini is all long strips and then discard the seeds. Use a spiralizer to ensure the strips are spaghetti-like.

2. Press the sauté function of your pressure cooker and once hot, add the oil and sauté the zucchini, cooking and stirring for a minute, until cooked through.

3. Transfer to the fryer basket. Place the basket on the trivet. Place the Crisp Lid on top of the inner pot and plug it in. Set to 350°F for 10 minutes. Season with some salt and black pepper. Enjoy with pasta sauce of choice.

Nutritional Information Per Serving

Calories - 182, Carbohydrates –12g, Fat – 14g, Proteins – 2g, Fiber – 4g, Cholesterol: 0mg

Crispy Kale Chips

Prep Time: 5 minutes

Cook Time: 3 minutes

Servings: 2

Ingredients

1 kale head

Cook spray

1 teaspoon soya sauce

Instructions

1. Remove the center steam of the kale and tear up into pieces of 1 ½ inches. Wash these pieces and dry.

2. Toss with the soya sauce and spritz with oil. Place in the basket. Set the Crisp lid trivet in the inner pot of your pressure cooker, place the fryer basket on top and set the Crisp lid on top of the inner pot. Plug in.

3. Cook at 450°F for 3 minutes, tossing halfway through. Enjoy!

Nutritional Information Per Serving

Calories - 27, Carbohydrates –3g, Fat – 1g, Proteins –1g, Cholesterol: 0mg

Grilled Cheese

Prep Time: 5 minutes

Cook Time: 10 minutes

Servings: 2

Ingredients

2 slices low carb bread

2 teaspoon butter

2 slices of American cheese

Instructions

1. Spread the butter on one side of each bread slice.

2. On the un-buttered sides, place the remaining ingredients and then place in the fryer basket. Place trivet in pot. Place basket on it. Set the Crisp Lid on the inner steel pot of the pressure cooker and plug in.

3. Cook 5 minutes on 360F, then flip and cook sandwich for 4-5 minutes until done.

Nutritional Information Per Serving

Calories - 367, Carbohydrates –17g, Fat – 27g, Proteins – 14g, Cholesterol: 80mg, Fiber –10g

Air Fried Blooming Onion

Prep Time: 20 minutes

Cook Time: 15 minutes

Servings: 2

Ingredients

1 large onion

2 tablespoons of milk

2 eggs

1 cup of almond flour

1 teaspoon of garlic powder

1 teaspoon of paprika

Olive oil

Instructions

1. Begin by peeling the onion and cut the top off, place side down and beginning from the root, cut the onion half inch downward. Cut to 8 slices all the way.

2. Place the onion in cold water, face down for 2 hours.

3. Combine flour and seasonings in a bowl and coat the onion thoroughly with the egg/ crumb mix. Now tip over to drip off excess. Sprinkle flour over the onion and place in the basket. Spray with cooking spray.

4. Set the Crisp lid trivet in the inner pot of your pressure cooker, place the fryer basket on top and set the Crisp lid on top of the inner pot. Plug in.

5. Cook for 10 to 15 minutes on 390°F.

Nutritional Information Per Serving

Calories - 406, Carbohydrates –20g, Fat – 25g, Proteins –22g, Cholesterol: 376mg

Air Fried Cabbage

Enjoy cabbage in a new yummy and deliciously crisp way!

Prep Time: 5 minutes

Cook Time: 10 minutes

Servings: 2-4

Ingredients

1 cabbage

Cooking spray

Bacon, optional

Parmesan

Instructions

1. Dice cabbage in large pieces and spray with cook spray.

2. Coat with bits of bacon, if using. Place in the fryer basket. Top with parmesan.

3. Set the Crisp lid trivet in the inner pot of your pressure cooker, place the fryer basket on top and set the Crisp lid on top of the inner pot. Plug in.

4. Cook at 375°F for 15 minutes.

Crispy Spinach

Prep Time: 5 minutes

Cook Time: 8 minutes

Servings: 2-4

Ingredients

½ bag baby spinach leaves

Cooking spray

1/8 teaspoon of garlic sea salt blend

Parmesan

Lemon juice

Instructions

1. Place in the fryer basket, not necessarily in a single layer, though. Spray with oil. Sprinkle with the blend.

2. Set the Crisp lid trivet in the inner pot of your pressure cooker, place the fryer basket on top and set the Crisp lid on top of the inner pot. Plug in.

3. Cook at 325F for 10 minutes.

4. Serve, sprinkle with parmesan and squeeze of lemon juice.

Nutritional Information Per Serving

Calories - 9, Carbohydrates –1g, Fat – 0g, Proteins –1g, Cholesterol: 1mg

Radish Hash Browns

Prep Time: 10 minutes

Cook Time: 15 minutes

Servings: 2-4

Ingredients

8 oz. radishes

1 small onion

1/2 teaspoon garlic powder

1/2 teaspoon granulated onion powder

1/4 teaspoon kosher salt

1/4 teaspoon paprika

Pinch freshly ground black pepper

Cooking spray

Instructions

1. Wash the radishes, cut off the roots, trim the stems but leave about ½ inch or less.

2. Slice the radishes and the onions and add to the fryer basket. Spray with oil and mix well.

3. Set the Crisp lid trivet in the inner pot of your pressure cooker, place the fryer basket on top and set the Crisp lid on top of the inner pot. Plug in.

4. Cook at 360F for 8 minutes, shaking twice. Add the seasonings to the basket and cook at 400°F for 5 minutes, shaking halfway.

Nutritional Information Per Serving

Calories - 52 Carbohydrates –7g, Fat – 0g, Proteins –2g, Cholesterol: 0mg

Spicy Cabbage

Prep Time: 5 minutes

Cook Time: 8 minutes

Servings: 2

Ingredients

½ teaspoon of crushed red pepper flakes

¼ teaspoon of cayenne pepper

1/8 cup apple juice

1/8 cup apple cider vinegar

1 carrot, grated

½ tablespoon of sesame seeds

1 cabbage, cut into 4 wedges

Instructions

1. Combine all the ingredients in the fryer basket.

2. Set the Crisp lid trivet in the inner pot of your pressure cooker, place the fryer basket on top and set the Crisp lid on top of the inner pot. Plug in.

3. Cook at a temperature of 350°F for 8 minutes.

Nutritional Information Per Serving

Calories - 111, Carbohydrates – 21g, Fat – 2g, Proteins – 5g, Fiber – 9g

Crispy Avocado Fries

Prep Time: 15 minutes

Cook Time: 10 minutes

Servings: 2-3

Ingredients

1 large avocados

Juice of 1lemon

1 egg whisked

½ cup blanched almond flour

½ cup parmesan cheese, grated

Cooking spray

Instructions

1. Peel the avocados, pit and slice into 3/4 inch thick wedges. Place the avocado slices in a bowl. Squeeze the fresh lemon juice them and toss to coat the slices evenly with the lemon juice.

2. Whisk the egg in a bowl. Pulse the almond flour and cheese together in a food processor and pour into a separate bowl.

3. Dip an avocado slice in the egg wash to coat, shake off excess egg drippings. Sprinkle the breading over the avocado slice, pressing to coat and stick. Place in a single layer in the fryer basket.

4. Set the Crisp lid trivet in the inner pot of your pressure cooker, place the fryer basket on top and set the Crisp lid on top of the inner pot. Plug in.

5. Cook at 375°F for 15 minutes and remove once it is crispy and golden brown. Serve, garnished with fresh cilantro.

Nutritional Information Per Serving

Calories - 240, Carbohydrates –11g, Fat – 18g, Proteins –10g, Cholesterol: 76mg

Scotch- Pork Ring Style Eggs

A delightfully decadent treat, air fried in your Crisp Lid, just for you!

Prep Time: 25 minutes

Cook Time: 15 minutes

Servings: 2-3

Ingredients

1 cup of water

3 large eggs

½ cup crushed pork rinds

1 egg, beaten

½ lb. ground pork sausage

Cooking spray

Instructions

1. Pour water into the pressure cooker's inner pot. Set trivet over the water and place the eggs on the trivet. Secure the lid and set the vent to the seal position. Cook on low pressure for 3 minutes and then perform a quick release.

2. Cool eggs in ice for a minute, peel and set aside.

3. In one bowl, place the crushed rinds; in another beat the egg. Divide sausage into 3 portions. Make a patty with each of the portions, place an egg in the center, and wrap the sausage around the egg to cover egg completely.

4. Dip each of the wrapped sausage in the beaten egg and then the pork rinds. Roll to coat on all sides. Spritz with cooking spray. Place in the fryer basket.

5. Set the Crisp lid trivet in the inner pot of your pressure cooker, place the fryer basket on top and set the Crisp lid on top of the inner pot. Plug in.

6. Cook at 390°F for 7 minutes. Flip and cook another 7 minutes. Remove to a rack to cool.

Nutritional Information Per Serving

Calories - 456, Carbohydrates –2.2g, Fat – 36g, Proteins – 31g, Cholesterol: 1006mg

Zucchini Chips

Exclusively air-fried in your Crisp Lid.

Prep Time: 10 minutes

Cook Time: 15 minutes

Servings: 2

Ingredients

Cooking spray

1 zucchini, sliced into coins

1/2 teaspoon of dried oregano

½ tablespoon of ranch seasoning

Sea salt

Freshly ground black pepper

Instructions

1. Place the zucchini in a large bowl. Add the oregano, ranch seasoning, salt, and pepper and toss.

2. Spritz the fryer basket lightly with cooking spray and then place the zucchini in it.

3. Set the Crisp lid trivet in the inner pot of your pressure cooker, place the fryer basket on top and set the Crisp lid on top of the inner pot. Plug in.

4. Cook at 375° for 12 minutes, flipping halfway through cooking.

Nutritional Information Per Serving

Calories - 21, Carbohydrates –3g, Fat – 10g, Proteins –1.5g, Fiber: 1g

Crispy Brussels Sprouts
Brussels sprouts are nutrient- packed, including omega-3 fatty acids, which is heart-healthy.

Prep Time: 5 minutes

Cook Time: 10 minutes

Servings: 2-4

Ingredients

1 lb. Brussels sprouts

1 tablespoon of coconut oil

Instructions

1. Remove loose leaves, cut in half and drizzle with oil.

2. Place in the fryer basket. Set the Crisp lid trivet in the inner pot of your pressure cooker, place the fryer basket on top and set the Crisp lid on top of the inner pot. Plug in.

3. Cook at 400°F for 10 minutes, flipping halfway. Brussels sprouts are cooked when tender and have darker caramelized spots.

4. Serve, drizzled with melted butter.

Nutritional Information Per Serving

Calories - 90, Carbohydrates –4.3g, Fat – 6g, Proteins –2.9g, Fiber: 3.2g

Balsamic Asparagus With Almonds

Prep Time: 10 minutes

Cook Time: 10 minutes

Servings: 2-4

Ingredients

1 bunch asparagus

2 tablespoon balsamic vinegar

Cooking Spray

Salt & pepper to taste

1/3 cup sliced almonds

Instructions

1. Place the asparagus on a plate, spritz with oil and balsamic. Sprinkle also with salt and pepper to coat asparagus completely. Add the sliced almonds.

2. Transfer to fryer basket and then place the basket on the trivet. Place the Crisp Lid on top of the inner pot and plug it in. Set to 350°F for 5 minutes; shake halfway through.

3. Enjoy immediately.

Nutritional Information Per Serving

Calories - 68, Carbohydrates –6, Fat – 4g, Proteins –3g, Fiber: 3g

Cheese Sticks

Prep Time: 10 minutes

Cook Time: 15 minutes

Servings: 2

Ingredients

2 eggs, whisked

2 tablespoons of almond flour

4 tablespoons of panko bread crumbs

1/3 cup grated parmesan cheese

12 oz. mozzarella cheese stick, halved &frozen

Instructions

1. Place the beaten egg in a bowl. Place the rest of the ingredients, except the cheese, in another bowl.

2. Dip the cheese stick in the egg and then in the flour mix. Once all is done, placed in a parchment lined cookie sheet. Do not overlap. Place in the freezer to freeze for at least 20 minutes.

3. Spritz the fryer basket with cooking spray. Working in batches, place the sticks in the basket. Place trivet in pot. Place basket on it. Set the Crisp Lid on the inner steel pot of the pressure cooker and plug in.

4. Cook 7 minutes for 375°F.

Nutritional Information Per Serving

Calories - 55, Carbohydrates –1g, Fat – 4g, Proteins – 4g, Cholesterol: 19mg, Fiber –1g

Air Fryer Biscuits

Prep Time: 15 minutes

Cook Time: 10 minutes

Servings: 8-9 small biscuits, for 2

Ingredients

1 cup almond flour

1/2 teaspoon baking powder

1/4 teaspoon kosher salt

1 cup cheddar cheese, shredded

2 tablespoons butter, melted

2 large eggs

2 tablespoons sour cream

Instructions

1. Combine in a large bowl, the almond flour, the baking powder, and the salt. Add the cheddar and mix by hand.

2. Add the butter, eggs, and the sour cream to the center. Mix until it forms a sticky batter.

3. Place a parchment paper in the fryer basket. Drop the batter on the parchment. (Work in batches). Place trivet in pot. Place basket on it. Set the Crisp Lid on the inner steel pot of the pressure cooker and plug in.

4. Cook at 400 F for 7-10 minutes, depending on the size.

Nutritional Information Per Serving

Calories - 167, Carbohydrates –3g, Fat – 15g, Proteins – 7g, Fiber –1g

Keto Onion Rings

Prep Time: 10 minutes

Cook Time: 15 minutes

Servings: 2-3

Ingredients

1 small or medium-sized onion, sliced into rings

1/8 teaspoon kosher salt

1 1/2 tbsp. coconut flour

1 large eggs

1/3 cup Pork rinds

1 1/2 tablespoons of blanched almond flour

1/4 teaspoon garlic powder

1/4 teaspoon paprika

Instructions

1. Combine the flour and salt in a bowl. In another bowl, beat the eggs and in a third, add together the almond flour, pork rinds, garlic powder and paprika, stirring well to mix all.

2. Dip an orange ring in the coconut flour and then the egg, shaking off excess. Coat with extra pork rind and place in the fryer basket.

3. Set the Crisp lid trivet in the inner pot of your pressure cooker, place the fryer basket on top and set the Crisp lid on top of the inner pot. Plug in.

4. Cook at a temperature of 400°F for 15- 20 minutes until golden.

Nutritional Information Per Serving

Calories - 135, Carbohydrates –8g, Fat – 7g, Proteins – 8g, Fiber –3g

Quick &Easy Air-Fried Asparagus

It only takes a few minutes and then you enjoy crispy asparagus sides. Healthy too!

Prep Time: 5 minutes

Cook Time: 10 minutes

Servings: 2- 4

Ingredients

1/2 bunch of asparagus, with bottom trimmed off

Cooking spray

Himalayan salt

Black pepper

Instructions

1. Place asparagus in basket and spritz with oil. Sprinkle with salt and pepper.

2. Set the Crisp lid trivet in the inner pot of your pressure cooker, place the fryer basket on top and set the Crisp lid on top of the inner pot. Plug in.

3. Cook 400°F for 10 minutes. Serve!

Roasted Broccoli

A really easy, fast and tasty dish!

Prep Time: 3minutes

Cook Time: 7 minutes

Servings: 2

Ingredients

2 cups fresh broccoli (about a pound), trimmed

Cooking spay

Sea salt & black pepper, to taste

Instructions

1. Place broccoli in basket and spritz with oil. Sprinkle with salt and pepper and toss to coat well.

2. Set the Crisp lid trivet in the inner pot of your pressure cooker, place the fryer basket on top and set the Crisp lid on top of the inner pot. Plug in.

3. Cook 400°F for 7 minutes. Serve!

Nutritional Information Per Serving

Calories - 61, Carbohydrates –6g, Fat – 4g, Proteins – 3g, Fiber –2g

The End

Printed in the USA
CPSIA information can be obtained
at www.ICGtesting.com
LVHW091218110724
785189LV00005B/362